Late Mowing

Poems and Essays by Stephen M. Holt

Stephen M. Holt

With an Introduction by
Kathryn Stripling Byer

Jesse Stuart Foundation
Ashland, Kentucky
2000

Acknowledgements & Special Thanks

Poems from this collection have appeared, sometimes in altered form, in the following journals: *Appalachian Journal, Belle's Letters Press, Jar, Midwest Poetry Review, Pikeville Review, Poetry Forum Journal, Potato Eyes, Roadrunner Press, Ship of Fools, South Ash Press, Sparrowgrass Poetry Forum, The Sun,* and *Sunflower Dream.*

"Jesse Stuart: A Reminiscence" first appeared in *Appalachian Heritage Magazine,* Winter 1991. "The Wurtland Merchants" was orginally printed, in different form, in *The Greenup News,* January 1983. "Eastern Woodlands: 1749" is scheduled to appear in *Now & Then* magazine, Vol.17, No.3 (Winter 2001). Copyright by Center for Appalachian Studies and Services, 2001. Used with permission. "A Place in Winter" first appeared in *Reviser's Toolbox,* a textbook by Barry Lane; Discover Writing Press, Shoreham, VT, 1999.

Special thanks to Stanley Ramey, Garnet Stafford, Dorothy Griffith and the late Bertha Savage: they lent me the books; to the staffs and participants of the 1998 and 1999 Appalachian Writers Conference at Hindman Settlement School; to my friends, for their generosity and interest; and to Wm.M. & Charlotte Adams Holt and the rest of my family, for their unfailing support.

Finally I would like express my gratitude to Michael McFee, Dr. Harry Brown, Dr. Robert J. Higgs, Linda Parsons Marion, and Marianne Worthington for their expertise, advice, and encouragement. Their approval of my writing has much to do with this book's having become a reality. Above all I must thank Kathryn Stripling Byer for being both mentor and friend.

FIRST EDITION

Copyright © 2000 by Stephen M. Holt. All rights reserved. No part of this book may be reproduced or utilized in any form or by any means without permission in writing from the publisher.

Library of Congress Cataloging-in-Publication Data
Holt, Stephen M., 1946-
    Late mowing : poems and essays / by Stephen M. Holt ; with an introduction by Kathryn Stripling Byer. -- 1st ed.
    ISBN 0-945084-87-0
    1. Appalachian Region--Poetry. 2. Appalachian Region--Civilization. 3. Mountain life--Appalachian Region. 4. Mountain life--Poetry. I. Title.
    PS3558.O422 L3 2000
    811'.6--dc21   00-048420

Cover Photo by Linda W. Holt
Book Design by Brett Nance

Published By: Jesse Stuart Foundation • P.O. Box 391 • Ashland, KY 41114 • (606) 325-2519

Contents

Introduction

POEMS: South Shore Seasons
    Part I   11
    Part II   25
    Part III   43
    Part IV   63

ESSAYS
    Jesse Stuart: A Reminiscence   81
    Under the Apple Boughs   87
    The Wurtland Merchants   91

DEDICATION

For Linda—faithful partner, honest critic
& in memory of
Margaret Roberson Holt & Estill Maggard—
they told me the stories.

And for Michael—
I will never forget your words about
my work; nor will your teaching and
critical ability go unappreciated.

My best always,
Steve
11/24/00

Introduction

When, in an interview several years ago, Irish Nobel Laureate Seamus Heaney described the poet as a voice box for the land and the people, he could have been speaking for the poets now writing out of the southern Appalachian mountains. Living in a region too long relegated to silence in the official literary history of this country, they have known the intimate relationship between voice and land, how one nourishes the other, how songs and stories help a people make it through hard times and isolation. Giving voice to our mountains, poets like Jesse Stuart, James Still, Jim Wayne Miller, Fred Chappell, Robert Morgan, Jeff Daniel Marion, and George Ella Lyon have helped to establish Appalachian poetry firmly in the ongoing story of American literature. Their Appalachia is as richly rendered as Heaney's Derry farmland. Read a Chappell poem like "Wind Mountain" aloud, for example, and its words seem to rise from the western North Carolina soil much as Heaney's "Broagh" and "Anahorish" seem to grow from the turf of northern Ireland.

Out of this Appalachian landscape comes *Late Mowing*, Stephen Holt's first collection of poems. Accompanied by three essays, the first of which, "Jesse Stuart: a Reminiscence," expresses the debt Holt owes to the man whose literary presence still lives in these mountains, its poetry introduces one of our region's most promising new voices. The book's title, with evocative ease, locates us right away in the country of this voice and suggests that Holt himself has come to his work late in his own season, something the reader begins to realize soon after the book's first pages.

And what a refreshing discovery that is, to find in the midst of our youth-obsessed culture the music of a mature voice discovering itself! For most of his adult life a teacher of literature, Holt did not attempt to write his own poems until his middle years. When he appeared in my poetry workshop at Hindman Settlement School two years ago, he responded to the first in-class writing with the memorable "That Time," memorable because the voice seemed to know, as if by instinct, how to make its way through the small universe of the poem and how (and when) to draw its lyric to a close.

As charmed as I had been by this introductory poem, nothing prepared me for the artistic growth in *Late Mowing*. A closer reading of Holt's work reveals his craftsmanship, including an almost painterly approach to the poem, the landscapist's perspective. Indeed, the title *Late Mowing* turns my mind toward the English landscape artists, particularly John Constable, a connection borne out by such poems as "How It Was" and "The Dead of Winter." Yet other poems like "Borderlands" and "Territorial" make me think of the Chinese landscape paintings of the S'ung Dynasty:

>Shadowy, slow-moving
>mountains surround
>the valleys of Virginia,
>where mists rise
>from undulant breasts
>sheened by rain
>and bright with sun
>as sea swells,
>past silver points of rock
>in the distant sky.
>   (from "Territorial")

Landscape pulses at the heart of these poems, and gathers together not only the natural world of the southern mountains, but the human and the historical, as well.

The word landscape itself suggests an artistic framework. As Simon Schama points out in his book *Landscape and Memory*, it entered the English language in the late 16th century, from the Dutch *landschap*, signifying a unit of human habitation, a part of the whole, framed by the act of measuring, of looking. And in that act of looking lies the artistry of Holt's poems.

Late Mowing's title poem shows his gift for paying attention; suggesting both landscape and still life, it bursts from the page in its color and suggestiveness: "This is the time of cobwebs strung like sculpted wire/On milkweed, wild aster & ironweed,/ Of cedar waxwings gorging on crops of chokecherries." Ripe with music, the vowels of this first stanza weave a texture of plenty, reminiscent of Keats' *Ode to Autumn*, even as its consonants tug and pull, creating a pleasurable tension of line and rhythm. The poem closes with the surprising image of garden slug, no more viscous than the oxheart tomato, as the poet reminds us, that "will now be salted & dissolved upon the spot, altogether// vanquished, unlike grandfather's hogs who always hung/Around as pink salt pork through winter,/ Or fleshy tomatoes sliced, salted & succulent on a skull-/White platter." The ability to express the mystery of fecundity and death through image, line, and syntax is the mark of a real poet. There is a playfulness in these lines that I admire. Grandfather's hogs hanging around through winter as salt pork and the linking of slug and succulent tomato! No reader is likely to forget the closure of this poem.

Thinking about Holt's landscape, the human occupation of it, I recall an encounter my husband and I had while hiking in the Rocky Mountain National Park several years ago. We passed a couple who, noticing my husband's Duke Basketball tee-shirt, stopped to chat. Learning that we were from the Smokies, they asked, "How do you like hiking in real mountains?"

Taken aback, my husband said, a shade defensively, "We think our mountains are just as real as these." Harmless as the comment was, it set met thinking. Real mountains. I puzzled over this for months afterward, setting our Blue Ridge against the Rockies. The difference was landscape, after all. Not that our mountains are any the less wild in places, but they have the mark of the human on them, whereas the Rockies more often do not. They are as much human habitation as they are rock, forest, or laurel hell, and they are rich in what Simon Schama calls the veins of myth and memory that lie beneath the familiar. Not surprisingly, the historical and the mythological pulse just under the surface of many of Holt's poems. In the last lines of "Territorial," Thomas Jefferson looks through his telescope, tracking wild geese through the "cool blue" at Buffalo Gap. Studying a dead rabbit in "Crossroads," the poet hears words from a blues song, dark and dusty as the life of Robert Johnson, "heading down the great length/ of shadowy womb/called the delta."

Ranging beyond Appalachian influences, Holt's poems reveal stylistic and thematic connections with other important contemporary American poets. For example, his lyricism invites comparison with that of Mary Oliver, whose lyrics, in their fluidity and clarity, have set the standard for contemporary nature poems. Holt's "September Realm," "Shroud in Blue," and "Long Dry Spell" are but three of the many poems with the same fluency of line and image. Moreover, Holt can, with a few well chosen details, sketch the emotional landscape of a poem as subtly as the the Chinese-American poet Li-Young Lee. Not to mention those ancient Chinese poets, Li Po and Tu Fu. He appreciates, as did they, the emotional weight of the image, and I would surmise that he has obviously learned much from Ezra Pound's masterpiece, *Cathay*, in which Li Po lives again, thanks to Pound's poetic re-creation of Chinese texts.

"Our limitations are our gateways to reality," the ever-quotable Flannery O'Connor once remarked. She also said, "The key word is see." With that key Stephen Holt continues the tradition of unlocking the Appalachian landscape, inviting his reader through the gate and into a reality brimming with history, song, and the ten thousand things of his keenly observed world.

Kathryn Stripling Byer
Cullowhee, NC
February 14, 2000

Part One

Flat, gray morning light,
and ice cracks down the valley
like a ringing bell.

Night Visitor

    Sometimes
    at night
    I feel
your satin slippers
    dancing away
    the numbness
from my slumbering
    palms,
    twirling
    like slender
threads and needles
    come to knit up
    the droplets
    moistening
    my hands
    as they cry
    for you
    in the hollow
    darkness.

Doe Lying Dead in the Snow

Red embroidery
on a white down comforter,
wind-frozen ruffles.

Eastern Woodlands: 1749

Winter camp at Lower Shawneetown. Snowflakes
thick as blanched corn seeds cover the earth
and the frozen Scioto, and cold indigo wind sweeps
bare the ridges, colors ravines.

On the banks of the river, wegiwas huddle like
ice-coated haybales. Bare white birch limbs shake
in the starkness of late afternoon as redbirds alight
to wait for the millet that spills down from baskets
to snowcrust.

In the focus of moonlight timberwolves wait
for the death-dance of deer through cornfield stubble.
Warriors wait for a break in the weather. To cross
the Ohio and enter the canelands.
> Trap for beaver.
> Work the salt licks.
> Trade furs as far as
> > Eskippakithiki.
> Raid for horses.

Softened and toughened as buckskin leather,
the women will wait in sharp vigil while the hunters
are gone. Soon they will pray with their hearts and
wait for a sign: comet crossing the sky, tail bright
as headdress feathers.
> Flaming Tecumseh.

Rising waters will blanket the floodplain,
drive this town to higher ground before he appears.
And a broad white surge will sweep them beyond
the red evening sun before he returns.

The Dead of Winter

1.
At Hanging Rock
steely rain spikes hard ground
like six-penny nails
from Fulton's Forge.

A hunched old hunter
wades through meadow slush.

Through mists
rise great stacks of fire-stained stone,
tombs of iron gods out of blast,
temple ruins in dark-branched hills.

2.
By the Falls of Pactolus,
Jesse Boone knelt, drank
and tasted salt, the residue of desire,
but he stayed on.

Dan'l had already fled
through a gap
toward the dim blue-stemmed plain,
not wanting history to lie here
and die.

BORDERLANDS

Winter here
is a mottled
carrousel horse
revolving blindly,
neighing silence,
deaf to a windsong.

We still ride.

Nerves of Steel

      Deep in this dark valley,
steel rails interstice
like raw nerves exposed
to bulling trains
that clutch and pound across them
every hour.

Wintering on the Russell Fork, Up Big Sandy

Dwellers in these hills are rooted and lean
as trees lining frozen banks,
and a cold meringue of haze
hangs from pine branches and rock ledges.

The skyline, high up,
is icy fingers having clawed up canyon walls,
suspending grief at least until a falsetto wind
flies it back down the narrows.

Such days as this, coals afire
light up the gorge
like a generous red mouth.

When I Awoke In Daybreak Fog

When I awoke in daybreak fog so thick,
                Cold
                Arched itself upon my sink
                And boldly laughed

While I, shaken, drew on
            One light green sock
                And one of gray

Then totally forgot to get
            The morning paper.

                I must cease this grieving
                          On your grief;
                          In brief,
        I know that you'll be fine
                          In time,

                          I think.

Commonwealth

    Eastern Kentucky fitfully slept
on the steps of Virginia's back porch.

    At Sycamore Shoals
Dragging Canoe told Boone himself
    "We have given you a fine land,
    but you will find it under a cloud,
    and a dark and bloody ground."

    How could the old chief
    have foreseen the time
when war would bloom in the coal fields?

Family Guest

At a time when the red fox
had almost vanished from our hills,
the old man sighted one
tripping down his hard-packed dirt lane
at first light
and shot her, had her stuffed and mounted
to grace the family guest room.

Of course they called her rabid,
those who considered
the metal in the Iron Curtain real as bricks
in the Great Wall of China, or
that having milk with fish
was certain agonizing death. Oh
she had to be destroyed, some said,
lest she sack our chicken coops, suck
down her silky throat those nest-egg fluids
we deserve for breakfast
and eat the fryers whose necks we mean
to wring for dinner.

And very likely she would have,
though her snarl flashed less fierceness
than startled unsureness
often found on faces trapped in tintypes.
Certainly no one would believe
she merely came to dip
her finespun paws and muzzle
in the icy meadow branch.

Anyway, time wore thin and dimmed
her scarlet coat, and she landed
in an attic or on some garbage heap,
I'm not sure which,
away from the gaze of every wary child
who feared at first the fine-edged teeth
polished like sunrise, then learned
to touch the soft trim of the tail,
then loved her like a sister.

A Place in Winter

For My Mother

The timepiece of night, coin-bright,
    Strikes the eternal moment,
    Shivers two brittle shadows
Like bones strewn upon the starkness.

The old man and his old hound
    Walk the icy fringe, again,
    To the boy who sleeps
Among the wind-licked stones.

Part Two

Lacing the hillsides,
with moonlight-painted faces:
slender dogwood trees.

How It Was

Morning in mid-March.

The pileated woodpecker,
passionate starving artist,
cleaves to the bark
of the honey locust,
etching & carving,
    etching & carving.

Out of hardwood hillsides
deer come like ghosts
to drink from the light
of the streams.
They flick their felt ears
    in the tracking wind.

Country men
from winter's outer dark,
weather-softened
as their worn brown fedoras,
mill on farm supply floors,
sift through barrels
    of seeds warm as stars.

Down from ridgetops,
silver-throated rain
splashes through cracks
in the cellar doors
    of shut-in wintry souls.

The Little Girls in the Photograph of the Old Wurtland School, 1901

Sweet as the rain dripping
from the black birch
onto their homecut bobs,
with faces sad and camera-frozen
as the rag dolls
dangling from their hands
like lost children, they stare,
old as the sandstone blocks
of the schoolhouse behind them
(or the sturgeon sleeping
in the river's muddy depths),
knowing the madcap boys
scrunched between them
will grow to be men
they might learn not to love.

Late Afternoon at Raceland Downs

Since being is motion,
    we clothe against the clumsy
        bear-hug winds of early March
            to walk the farm pond trace,
poplar-rimmed. Icicles flash
    from brittle branch
        'til silky night gowns
            naked fields, and distant
houses fade like footprints
    in the depths of summer.
        Because motion is change.

The Ohio: Ancient Myth

Sliding past
           the streams
    that feed her

the monstrous
           flickering
           river
     slithers
south

devouring
her own children
    as
    she

         goes.

April Then

Walk with me
    When downriver winds
        Ruffle maples to silver,
Chasten sycamores
    Clean as white lines
        Of a woman's fresh wash.
When dark alluvial ferns
    Lap like tongues
        At clear, cleansing rains.

Jesus Wept

      It was Jesus,
                    and He stopped traffic for the crowd
                  to offer them all fillet-o-fish sandwiches.
But they began shouting, "Christ!" Can't we have fries too?"
      and when He said, "I really don't think fries would be
                good for you, couldn't I just get
                you salads instead?"
          they began to stab Him
          with plastic forks and knives
          'til He fled
          across the bridge into southern Ohio.

Recovery from the Breaks at Elkhorn City

This healing time
is slow,
like a long coal train
heaving
toward a tunnel
deep in these mountains,
or 3 a.m.,
before night birds
first begin
to sing the gorge
to daylight;
3 a.m.,
when a man's cry
carries
a long way
without being heard.

Battle Cry

Wandering Shiloh Battlefield,
I saw in a small ravine the very spot where
General Albert Sidney Johnston, C.S.A.,
bled to death. I thought of the woods
on Uhlan Branch where my brother and I
used to play cowboys and war games
with cornstalks for weapons.

One tiny minié bullet ripped through an artery
to fill Johnston's boot with sparkling red blood
before a surgeon could even arrive...
The finest soldier in the whole Rebel army.
Lost.

My brother, on the other hand, was never
to my knowledge physically wounded
in Southeast Asia. Although he says he was.
That he received a Purple Heart, but threw it
angrily into the China Sea before he came home.

Recently he was strapped down in a St. Louis
hospital and given a shock treatment.
Now he is very gentle and quiet. At night
I hear him creep about the house.
He whimpers in cowboy pajamas...
The finest lancer along all of Uhlan Branch.
Lost.

That Time

behind the little house
beneath the hill
I climbed upon
the lawn chair's arm,
checked the Cannon towel
fastened around my neck
by a safety pin,
looked out
across the gravel road
to the distant town,
and flew.

Into a crawdad hole.
Ankle sprain.

Short flight.
That time.

Stand Scotland Where It Did?
Macduff—Macbeth (IV.iii)

The river foothill beyond my house
Used to look so much like Scotland.
Now it's a course for playing at golf:
        A Scottish game, at least.

Morning Coffee

My mind's a matting cloud of dust,
    a swirling gray pillar of doubt.
I give a shake to clear it out:
    Half-memories of things done.
        Or undone.
    Whole ones of things said.
        Or unsaid…

I see the brown-streaked finch
    is singing from a ragged tuft
        of crabgrass in the yard.

Highland Bluebird

In her loneliness
has she flown beyond starlight?

Lithely she fashions
a fragrant, finespun nest
in a seasoned cedar fence row
    along an open meadow,
a nest much too close to the earth.

Too close to the cunning
    of bushytailed foxes,
too near the silence of serpents,
    too near the preying of friends
        in the fields.

May her bright wings
    redeem her.

One Morning in May

Rain kisses rooftops
as earth invites to depths
wet whorls of rooted grass.

Territorial

Shadowy, slow-moving
mountains surround
the valleys of Virginia,
where mists rise
from undulant breasts
sheened by rain
and bright with sun
as sea swells,
past silver points of rock
in the distant sky.

Through the telescopic glass
in his observatory tower,
Jefferson tracks wild geese
winging through the cool
blue at Buffalo Gap, wonders
what must lie beyond &
who should go
when it comes time.

Meriwether Lewis at Grinder's Trace

Tangled in the forest, the details
hang like grapevines. Maybe someone
pulled the wool over his eyes and shot.

Whoever found him, slack as the ropes
of his tavern bed, kept the news under wraps,
let the logs on the fire cool to charcoal.

Anticlimax anyway, since Jefferson
once assumed him dead and gone
in a changing moon of one long rocky season.

Perhaps those days had slowed
and dragged him deep as mules' hooves
sucking spring mud in west Tennessee.

Or surfeit of plenitude, so much teeming
did him in: journals full of endless space,
tribal tongues, great beasts to be used up.

At last he must have felt whittled down
like a poplar stick shaped into a whistle
shrill as wolf tones on the Beaverhead.

Still he had lived to shudder at what Keats
could only imagine, the cold hard blues
of sky and sea converged on a faraway coast.

Crossroads

I found
in the middle
of a crossroads
a dead young rabbit.
Laying him
in the long grass
under locust
and sycamore trees,
I thought
how light he is,
and no longer than
a syllable,
then I heard
the words
from a blues song
dark and dusty
as the life
of Robert Johnson
heading down
the great length
of shadowy womb
called the delta.

Part Three

Bird baths go dry.
Softening doves perch upon
powerlines, silent.

Sawmill Hollow: A Revisitation

1

                Clarity and awareness
in this forgotten groove between two slopes,
    where I become instinctual and human.

2

                Outcrops jut from shale.
The glacier, great northern cat,
crept down here, flicked frost-rimmed paws
at the hills, must have felt the heat
                        and backed away.

3

                A red-tailed hawk stares
from a blanched-out sycamore branch. A pair
of fawns flash through the creek,
cattails and water willows flagging its border.
The meadow wears Queen Anne's lace,
        and cornflowers grace her hair.

4

    Sunken tracks. Lather of oxen, grease
of old wagons, the scent of shavings curled
from hickory and oak, smooth-planed:
                I begin to know myself
as one not here to claim this ground
        except as a place to come home to.

5

    I will climb up in these woods to die,
high among dark ferns where lizards sleep
    above the surprising blue of cornflowers.

Forbidden Fruit

     Blackberries: Jeweled ladies.
Round and firm. Ripe. Aching
To be baked in their own dark sweetness.

     Salt on my tongue.
Sweat on my fingers. Gently I open
Their cluster of vines. Softly I enter
Their most private places.

     Copperhead: Underworld king.
Awaiting first sparrows. Baiting with berries.
Only his soul ever slumbers.

Summer Morning Rising

Pleased with the burial of another yesterday,
    the sun is waking thirsty, stealing along
    the powdered, crooked pathway.
Dust on the larkspur by empty barns,
    dust on vines in the arbor,
    firestones in the dust.
The Spanish daggers of pearl rain
    will not come here today.
Ah! but the thicket's full of huckleberries,
    copious wine decanters,
        and you and I shall pluck and talk
        'til purple spills over our pails.

Shoeing the Roan

For Chester W. Harris

    Years ago, when I was the paperboy,
I stopped on my route to watch your grandfather
shoe a roan stallion. He cradled its back left hoof
in one hand, drove iron into horn with the other,
burnt up the air.
              It was lightning striking flintrock.

                        The horse's
ears stood at the ready, and his eyes weren't even
blinking in the sunlight.

    Some fellow walked over to ask a question,
or to comment, and the roan snorted, then jerked
and shifted all three freestanding legs left to right.
His entire weight.
              Your granddad gripped foreleg
and fetlock, bore the whole heft and movement
without a flinch. Went on talking just as cool as
the waterbucket.

Now what would such an animal scale out at:
eight, nine hundred pounds? I tell you it takes
a strong person to support somebody when they
shift their whole weight against him.

                        Looking back,
it strikes me as curious how the other man never
changed his expression through all that. Maybe
he never knew enough about horses, or blacksmiths,
to recognize what he'd witnessed.
                     Either that
or he'd seen it done before.

Precious You Are to Me

Warm as the nostrils of fawns
    in the dark pine forest.
Fragrant as leaves of lemon balm.
Delicate as violin strings your mouth.

Yet you are sharp as lava beds.
Or Durango tequila.

If you were one of ten thousand
    Pamlico ponies
    grazing the seaboard marshes,
    I would know you.

I would pick you out.

Searching Through the Forms of Things

By day the aching sun
flicks its long tongue against my cusp of skin,
while in silence under stones and wood
I listen for connections.

                Come the arc of night,
someone tilts the dipper, pouring molten glow
into a cooling sky that shapes and scatters
all the glassy ingots, as far away as words
                    last time we tried to talk.

Elwood Adams, Retired, In His Workshed

Shaping an order from cedar freshness,
Elemental and clean, its good flesh
Pulsing with warmth in his hands,
He bleeds away sawdust,
Joins the bones of boards &
Hooks to chains the finished swing,
Another hanging basket.

He knows folks who come to buy
Will plant themselves, grow bright
As afternoons on Tygart's Creek.

Voices

The town boys used to climb
the tower on Beacon Hill,
seventy-five feet up, in wind
that swayed the ladder as if
it rocked a sleepy, fretful child.

Killer T. could hook his legs
over the top rung, hang
upside down in the stiff surge,
thump his chest and yell
full-throated and clear
to the river, like Tarzan.

One day at his trick,
Killer's legs slipped.
Brusquely he fell to his death.

His startled yawp trailed off
like a wound-down siren…
so weak no one in town
even barely heard it.

But when they led his mother
up to his broken body, and
she fell forward to embrace it,
cracked and runny as an eggshell,
tiny and soft as an embryo,
we clearly heard the silence
pouring through the shattered
oval of her mouth.

Clearing

My breath brittled
like a dry twig:

A yearling stepped out
of a deep wood
into the clearing,
his scent green as pines.

His eyes shone like planets
as he eased
tender grass blades
from the palm of my hand.

Some days I think
we're not often alone
in this uneasy world.

The Watch

Last night as my wife
came up from the garden,
a tiny robin fell from its nest
into our back yard.

As August's sun heats up,
the mother sits on a wire
and keens for her child, or
flies down to keep it from cats
or to feed it.

No woman whose darlings
were stranded at sea
could care for her babies
a bit more than she.

In Stillness Lie

Listen, my love: the breeze.
The night breeze
bends low toward the plain
to fondle the blonde fields
of wheat—your hair
being loosened and kissed.

Earth Poem

When I die,
let me sleep in her hands.

Her palms,
two cupped shells of pearl
where I drink a deep song.
Petals of morning glory
unfold at daybreak
to float on their surface.

The stoneground wheat
is in love. Caressed
by her sun-warmed fingers,
soon it will rise into loaves.

Who has known her
and not known the touch
of her hands? Or ever felt
death in the room?

When I die,
let me sleep in her hands!

The Solitary Keeper

Touched by afternoon wind,
her hair flowed like harp strings
as she held high her clinging wet dress
and piper-like
gathered mussel shells from creek shoals,
lugged a bucket through oozing mud flats
and up the steep bank toward home.

Yet how transitory her nature like a star:
to the veranda comes sundown,
and a glass harmonium's fragile resonance
betrays her position like a firefly.
White table, white chair,
and lemons steeped pure in sunlight.
A clay goblet sweating cool beads,
a rose weeping burgundy droplets.

I know she seeks a proper rider
for her sleek dream of Bluegrass stallions
come to life from bronze sculpture
to prance around her on marble tiles.

Graveyard at Boone Furnace

Two hundred years. Still, change
Rides horseback past this ground.
Trace Fork winds a leaden sheet
Through creekgrass. Sunfires glance
Off marble veins of earth and sky.

Wolfe. Whitt. Kehoe. Boggs. Bear.
Hard names of weathered clans
Who plowed the dirt they lie in.
Halfway Hollow. Head of Grassy.

Brother crow, black-frocked
Old preacher, lights on a headstone,
Leads the flock in a phlegmy hymn.

Advance Scouting in Northeast Kentucky

       Striking quick as a war party,
the flat bronze snout deeply sank
like an arrowhead into heavy flesh
that trod upon the body coiled thickly
asleep in a canebrake.

       The sun ran copper on creekwater
while an X from Simon Kenton's knifeblade
drained black venom from Dr. John Wood's
calf muscle. For three cautious days roaring
mosquitoes and deerflies, eager for blood
as cattle for salt blocks, raided sweating
coonskin heads and the swollen wound.

       Meanwhile, Michael Tygart
wandered off and saw in coves the emerald
shield of Ireland where a long time ago
a walking saint quenched the fires of serpents,
and on lookingglass waters cloudshapes
of cows bent toward Johnson grass, beehives,
hogs in their pens, tobacco barns. Ignoring
the likenesses of moccasin tracks and ears
of Shawnee maize vivid as war paint, he
christened both stream and valley TYGART'S
and settled in.

       But no matter.
Thrown one night from his horse,
he drowned in his own twisting creek:
tortuous reminder of the names of all
the things that had been there before him.

Long Dry Spell, 1932

Over and over
the dark sky displayed its moon,

a white-gold bowl
of liquid promise.

Slow and merciless heat
slipped inside bodies,

thickened the breath of despair,
melted souls like candlewax;

cracked our containers,
set our ceilings on fire;

dried out the greenwood curtain,
withered crops on the vine;

shrank apples, worried them
into roadside baths of dust.

The hungry came and ate,
cores and all.

Up Dark Hollow

Deflected by quartz
    in the cliff walls,
Pierced by the cattails
    in ponds:

    August moon.

Warning Signs

      Friday a sober groundhog,
shunning the weight and crunch
of my footsteps, rumbled
into the safety of horseweeds.
He knows my race.

      Yesterday a chipmunk,
spinning hard in the path
of my car's tires, was yanked
down a bank on a piece of string
nature had tied to his leg.

      Below my evening window
sits a cicada, haggard old prophet
setting a bow to his strings.
First time he has dedicated to me
the annunciation, first letting
of the lifeblood of summer.

Part Four

Three yellowjackets
swimming in an open keg
of fresh, sweet cider.

September Realm

How good it was,
in the gold glint & apple scent of autumn,
to lie back in tall grasses
among scattered hulls of fallen black walnuts.
To listen…

Tracking the banks of Kinnikonnick Creek,
two young beagles blew mellow horns
while I heard the old stories,
my ears keen as a wild hare's.

L'ombre

1.
I pass through
the iron gates
of night,
scan the cold sky
for the stars.
Bright steppingstones
where God
takes His walks.

2.
At nighttime
only crickets
singing,
only cloudshapes
dancing.
On the horizon
the shallowest stars,
almost on dry sky-shore,
almost on dry ground.
Ah! If I could reach
those near flagstones,
could touch their
bright surface, smell
their gold odors.

3.
In the absence
of starlight
the river of sky
runs deeper.
Earth's blackness, blacker.

In the silence
we silently pray.
Talk is the sound
of a fear of the skies.
At daybreak we talk—
Softly:
the heavens are sleeping.
Should we disturb them?
How to address them?

4.
Fence posts and man
go mad
from their shadows
by day
moving around them,
circling, circling.
Our shadows are ghosts
of the night.
L'ombre means shadow.
El hombre means man.

Reflection at Bennett's Mill Bridge

        Dark, pulsating waters
flow below this weathered tunnel
like blood. I do not search
for any shimmering image of my own,
but for yours.
                Sheltered like fossils
in strata of shale, we must come free
as seasoned leaves to follow the current,
with only the shadows of wild birds and bridges
to give us pause.

Late Mowing

This is the time of cobwebs strung like sculpted wire
        On milkweed, wild aster & ironweed,
Of cedar waxwings gorging on crops of chokecherries.

I swear sometimes the end of summer's a relief from
        Drooping fruit & vegetable fullness.
Fall's a woman tired from the strains of heavy labor.

September, we take to houses. But the laggard slug
        Who crawled onto a damp back porch
And sleeps in someone's garden shoe is strange, &

Though really no more viscous against the skin than, say,
        The flesh, wet pulp of an oxheart tomato,
Will now be salted & dissolved upon the spot, altogether

Vanquished, unlike grandfather's hogs who always hung
        Around as pink salt pork through winter,
Or fleshy tomatoes sliced, salted & succulent on a skull-
        White platter.

Aunt Maggie Speaks from the Rest Home

No one likes to look at an old woman's skin.
Old skin hangs like Christ on the cross
of a body, smells like a riverbank cabin.

Once mine was softened by lotions, gentled
in lovemaking; then came too many years
in the washroom, redness from bleach burns
and gritty Boraxo.

My skin is a wallpaper covering, flecked
brown by age spots, laced in blue
creeping veins, stretch-marked
from the long sag of birthings; cracked
from too many garden-hoe seasons of sun,
dried out as the drought-ridden earth.

Thin as a moth's wing in lamplight
my skin; light as a granddaughter's laughter,
airy but coarse as the snakeskin a grandson
discovers and brings in from play.

Come evening I draw down the skin
of my eyelids, shades to shut out the light.
To bring on the night. To shut out the light.

My god, I am ready to shed this old skin.

Appalachian Eve

October's end.
    Blooms have faded, fallen,
        fled their slender stalks.
Sundown's wind
    pipes o'er leaves
        dry as skins of serpents.
They shake their dusty heads,
    mumble in the dusk of old time.
Foxes rise from their dens,
    bark on yawning hills.
The moon looms like a lord
    above branches of wild plum trees.
From deep in the room
    you light up the walls
        like pure foxfire.
Forest shadows create night's design.
    My hymn of praise to thee I line:
        "O Love, O Love! I am thine."

Leaving the Cemetery
on Uhlan Branch

        How foreboding
the convergent lean of willows
on this neglected creek in late spring,
where grape hyacinth scents the wind
        before rain, clouding meanings.

        Three ponies from the pasture,
alert & somehow fazed, grazed in wild fescue
as we contemplated dates on family gravestones
        sleeping in light on the hilltop.

        Sometimes we are reminded
of the sharp pain of being born,
        the exacting levy for living.

Shroud in Blue

Time's housekeepers
Rearrange all things past,
Or sweep them completely
Out his back door,
Except for a cedar-scented chest
He once hand-fashioned
For his fancy lady (though he knows
She is often unfaithful).

Inside it, safe in a corner,
Rest the mementos of our intimacy.
They are so fragile,
Sad and beautiful as lilies,
Warm as Indian summer,
Fine as bracelets of clover.
Shrouded in powder blue linen,
They sleep.

Great Yellow Hound

For My Father

The morning they put Ol' Dinah away
she dozed by the sideyard swing,
caught again the western wind
across stone-marked ground,
led the chase.

Led, bone-stiff, to the orchard slope,
she reared her cocked head
toward the last sharp yaps
from wild November fields.

One neat shot between earth-brown eyes,
and she settled down into her mother.

The Old Shepherd Pauses Beside Savage's Pond

A deep green blanket
of wind-wrinkled water

cradles an evening moon
in this long-bearded place.

Slight gasps from leaves
surprised on the footpath:

>two lovely girls
>fresh from the orchard,

>lush manes
>brushed aureate gold,

>hooves soft as
>snow in the forest.

The Old Shepherd Becomes Tangled in a Friend's Sad Ballad

Such a high lonesome sound!
Dark as howls on the mountain.

Now the wild cherry shies
from cold plaits of white rain

that whiplash cattle over sedge,
rush small birds to paltry cover,

and I fight the wet windsweep
to fill for you

this burnt-orange basket
with wildflowers.

Crop Circles

I would like it to be
some late-Victorian farmer
who rouses his drowsy old plowhorse
under an ashen moon at midnight,
clinches her to a clacking wooden reaper
and turns her around the grain fields
in pure geometric precision
while a gathering of angels,
creamy faces resting in plump hands,
peers over the dreamy edge of heaven
delighted with the revelation below
and resolved to renew,
after a short nap,
the longtime survey of Loch Ness
and its deep, strange waters to the north.

Change on Whetstone Creek

1.

White-armed sycamores,
their light leaves removed
like gloves furred by dust
in a crackling season.

2.

Wild chicory, yellowroot
& the down-swing glint
of a scythe blade.

3.

When the first cold wind
combs the high meadow,
parts its frosted hair pale
as stone or dead fire, I
will go from these hills again.

4.

And what from this ground
shall I keep?

Cry of wild geese,
scent of wood smoke,
quick melt of snow on my face.

Essays

Jesse Stuart: A Reminiscence

Hold April when there's music in the air,
When Life is resurrected like a dream,
When wild birds sing up flights of windy stair
And bees love alder blooms by the stream.

—— Jesse Stuart, "Hold April"

Growing up in the Ohio River foothills near Greenup, Kentucky, I early became aware of Jesse Stuart's reputation as a significant American author. Of course as a child I read several of his books, such as *Red Mule* and *Penny's Worth of Character*, and I also caught an occasional glimpse of the man himself strolling down Main Street in Greenup, shaking hands and always talking. An imposing, square-shouldered man with a firm jaw and warm, alert eyes, his presence seemed to envelop the entire town. As my interest in literature increased, my interest in Jesse Stuart increased until I became acquainted with him in the mid-1960s.

I cannot say that Jesse supplied the sole impetus for my attempting a college education, or becoming a teacher, or writing my first poem. But I can certainly say he influenced me greatly in each of those endeavors. He was an important influence and role model, and his inspirational example during the days of my young adulthood gave me much confidence in the years just ahead. In fact, I have come to realize how very fortunate I am to have been in the presence of such a remarkable artist and educator as Mr. Stuart, a man who always proudly sang his tales in a lyrical, affirmative, refreshing voice that strengthened my connection to my native ground and helped me better understand where I fit within that place.

My fondest memories of Jesse are those from springtime, the season he loved and praised so much. To him, the rebirth phase of the seasonal cycle is most precious. Aware, no doubt, of T.S.

Eliot's famous paradoxical assertion in *The Waste Land* that "April is the cruellest month," Jesse writes in the ninth of his sonnet series *Man With a Bull-Tongue Plow*,

> Oh, April is the fairest month, to us—
> White flowers in the silver blowing wind—
> And their leaves in the wind hang tremulous
> And wind and leaves play a sweet violin.

Indeed, it is in spring, particularly in April, that I am most often reminded of this proud Scots-Irish son of the Appalachian soil.

In the spring of my senior year at the old Wurtland High School, "Miss Lutie" Nickell, a remarkable septuagenarian English teacher, struck upon the idea of presenting the dramatic version of Jesse's autobiographical novel *The Thread That Runs So True* as our school play. The night of the performance, there we were—an elderly lady and a handful of unskilled but willing teenagers on the stage of our cavernous high school gymnasium, presenting a play inspired by the work of a renowned author, with that very author seated in the audience, watching intently from his metal folding chair near the free throw line of the gym floor.

I had taken the minor role of a student of Jesse's 1925 Lonesome Valley School, and I recall having a mere seventeen lines to deliver. But I delivered each line with a full heart; indeed, our entire cast responded with real effort, and after the curtain call Mr. Stuart lavished praise upon the production. He noted enthusiastically, "You young people have marvelous speaking voices—very well-modulated, and they carry so well." I considered this comment high praise because Jesse's own voice had the same qualities he had attributed to ours.

In fact, with each reading of Jesse's works, I unfailingly hear his powerful voice echoing like a fox hunter's horn across a cold Kentucky ridge in December. I hear it clearly when I read in *The Thread That Runs So True*,

> I thought if every teacher in every school in America—
> rural, village, city, township, church, public or private—could
> inspire his pupils with all the power he had, if he could teach

them as they had never been taught before to live, to work, to play, to share, if he could put ambition into their brains and hearts, that would be a great way to make a generation of the greatest citizenry America ever had...

At the conclusion of my senior year I saw Jesse Stuart again, this time at the home of his good friend, Ben Webb, my high school principal. My father and I had arrived to help Mr. Webb pack for a move to a new principal's position in southeastern Ohio; a moving van had been backed up to the porch of the Webb's home, with Ben and Jesse sitting on the porch, ostensibly waiting for us all to go to work. On our first trip into the house Jesse selected a living room lamp and I picked up the end table beneath it. That was also our last trip. As we deposited the items in the back of the van, Jesse turned abruptly and asked, "Young man, are you interested in the Greeks?"

"Well, yes, I guess I am," I bemusedly replied.

"Then sit down here and let me tell you about the Greeks," he commanded, pointing to the back porch. "Wonderful people, the Greeks. They remind me of the people right here in Greenup County. They do things, they get things done!"

Thus, while my father and Mr. Webb were "getting things done," Jesse began a fascinating, lengthy monologue regarding the works of Homer, Xenophon, and Plato, the Battle of the Plain of Marathon, the Battle of Salamis, and any other possible subject dealing with the ancient Greek civilization. His jaw set firmly and his eyes alive and snapping, Jesse rendered his glorious account of those times. Neither of us seemed to notice that Ben Webb and my father had continued steadily working until the van was loaded. They never once interrupted Jesse, and I am sure they recognized exactly what was occurring—Jesse Stuart was teaching, beyond the classroom—and they realized the value of the experience to both the master teacher and the fledgling scholar. Late afternoon had yielded to the darkness of the early spring evening when Jesse finally turned over his ancient tale to the myriad frogs and crickets in the surrounding pastureland.

During my sophomore year at Eastern Kentucky University, Professor James Mangus, a wry world literature teacher, became aware of my Greenup County past, and occasionally, with a kind of sardonic interest (or admiration), he would link my Jesse Stuart connection to his lectures. For example, while mentioning the reluctance of the Greek tragedians to portray violence on the stage, Mangus cleared his throat, paused, stared straight at me, and said, "But of course Mr. Holt, being from Jesse Stuart's dark and bloody country, and being a close associate of Mr. Stuart's, will no doubt have difficulty relating to such ethical considerations." Then he added, "You do know Mr. Stuart quite well, Mr. Holt?"

Having no idea what else to do, I elected to consider Mr. Mangus' remarks as oddly complimentary.

One Friday afternoon near the semester's end, and just as Jim Mangus rounded the corner and headed toward those of us awaiting the start of class, the elevator across the hall opened and out strode Jesse Stuart, freshly arrived on campus for one of his visits as author-in-residence. Truly this was the moment of reckoning for me: should Jesse not acknowledge me, Jim Mangus would certainly acknowledge that the writer had not. But Jesse looked at me, hesitated, broke into a broad smile of recognition, and exclaimed "Holt!" Firmly grasping me by the shoulder, he turned toward Mangus and boomed, "This boy's grandfather was the best blacksmith in Greenup County! Why, he could get dead drunk, shoe your horse, guarantee those shoes for five years, and five years later that horse would pass by on the street wearing those same shoes. That's the kind of blacksmith Archie Adams was. I put him in one of my books, as a matter of fact."

Jesse then turned and briskly moved off down the hall to his destination, leaving Mr. Mangus to admit, with mock reluctance, that I did indeed know the man well. What he perhaps still did not recognize, and what I had just realized, was that Jesse Stuart knew me far better than I knew him. With his uncanny ability to remember local family names and histories, he had spontaneously created a mythic image of my grandfather stoutly plying his trade like a 1930s Hephaestus.

In the spring of my senior year of college, Ben Webb and I visited Jesse and his gracious wife Naomi at the old Stuart homeplace, a finely-kept log house nestled in a cove of W-Hollow near Greenup. That visit began with another of Jesse's sermons on the admirable qualities of the Greek civilization, delivered while a recording of Greek folk musicians played in the background of the sitting room. The visit ended with Jesse proudly showing us the interior of the utility building at the foot of the hill sloping down near the back of the house. The shelves inside were stacked with every original manuscript of poem, short story, or novel that he had written.

Opening a box containing an ink manuscript, complete with deletions and additions, that he had written years earlier, Jesse delivered a second sermon for the day. Placing that original story in my hands and watching me carefully cradle it, a chrysalis before it had taken wings and flown, he said, "Writing is hard work, no matter what you might be led to think. It isn't enough just to have the story come from inside you—why, that's when the real work begins. That's when you must gain control of the thing. Even when the start is fast, the finish can be a long way off. You have to really want to write to do it well."

I was reminded of a story Ben Webb had told me. While Jesse was recuperating from one of a series of heart attacks, the Stuarts and Webbs had taken a tour of North Africa and the Middle East. Under doctor's orders to relax completely, Jesse had instead been lecturing at public schools and universities almost every day. Deep into night, inside their tents, the others would often be awakened by the peck, peck, pecking of Jesse at this typewriter, creating and perfecting—driven to write, regardless of health.

As the years have passed, and especially since Jesse Stuart's passing in 1984, I have better been able to place him and his work in a satisfactory perspective. It seems to me that Jesse's propensity for the Greeks holds a key to one's understanding of him. His Greece was not the dark, primitive place of the uncompromising gods in classical tragedies. On the contrary, Jesse Stuart's world is more akin to the Greek point of view in the Golden Age of the fifth century B.C.. His own personality as well as his work emphasizes the freedom to develop oneself in a world of perpetual curiosities, and his essential insistence upon the truly democratic elements in society and his vision of man's great possibilities are ever-present in his writing.

Clearly Jesse Stuart thrived on the camaraderie and open-air atmosphere around the courthouse square in his beloved Greenup, a place of farmers, politicians, and business people—his personal Athenian gathering place. He loved to talk to his people and he loved their talk in turn. Endowed with a Southerner's strong sense of place, he neither forgot nor deserted his people. His strong sense of belonging would never have allowed him to accept a view of a fragmented modern world. Instead, the essence of his world could be found on Saturday morning in town in the spring of the year, with the very scent of renewal emanating from the moisture of the ground itself.

It has been said that we all have a story to tell. If that is so, I am surely grateful that as a young man I had the privilege of listening to Jesse while he told parts of his story and of reading the books in which he told the rest.

So when the serpentine waters of Lower Tygart and the Little Sandy try on their brand new mantles of cool maple and sycamore shade while sliding across the smoky valleys of early spring, and when cattle and horses plunge eager nostrils into light-green, sweet meadow salads of clover, then from the shadows of the silver dogwood hillside and out of the gray mask of dusk rising from the antique creek bank looms the voice of Jesse Stuart, Greek-spirited poet and teacher of Greenup County, Kentucky.

Under the Apple Boughs

"Now as I was young and easy under the apple boughs..."
—— Dylan Thomas, "Fern Hill"

When I was very young, my immediate environment comprised my whole universe. My father's job on the C & O Railway often kept him away from home day and night, so vacations or long-distance traveling of any sort were simply not part of our family routine. The early evenings of most fair-weather days I spent with my mother, younger brother and sister in the front porch swing, where we turned our heads and followed every automobile that came up or down U.S. 23. Sometimes, for enhanced recreation, we counted cars. The whole neighborhood did.

Within the confines of my world were, across the road and to the right, Arnold Lewis' barbershop and Speck Chinn's garage, as well as Lorraine Tufts' service station. Arnold was an old man with a white mustache and wooden leg. He had to sit on a stool attached to his barber chair so he could make it through a workday. Speck and Lorraine were brother and sister. He had a gold tooth and chewed on an unlit cigar while he repaired cars, always talking to customers through the cigar instead of removing it from his mouth. She was a biology teacher and businesswoman who always wore pants. Her husband Smokey, a bear of a man, ran the station.

To the left and on our side of the street were two stores: patriarch Wurts Chinn's General Merchandising, Est. 1910, and Edgar Long's Grocery. Wurts and his wife Addie were renowned in the community for having allowed hungry, jobless families to purchase food on credit during the Great Depression without ever demanding that anyone pay them back, even when times improved. Edgar was a giant of a man whose kindness and affability matched his size. His laugh carried loud and long.

Behind our house ran the railroad tracks. My parents had declared them off limits to me, for good reason, of course. Across the road stood Don Rice's apple orchard, a lovely, fenced-in acre bulging, in season, with Rome Beauties and Jonathans. Another forbidden place.

"Don't ever get over into Don Rice's field," my mother would caution me. "That would be trespassing."

Having no desire to begin a life of crime, I had complied. Still, the orchard fascinated me. In summer it was green and red, then gold in the evening light, cool and tempting to a boy who had been playing baseball all day in the hot sun.

Occasionally I saw Don Rice deep in his orchard, spraying his trees, a straw hat pulled low over his forehead blocking his eyes from the sun. He was the only adult in the neighborhood whom I did not know personally. Everyone else treated me as if I were special, as if I were a clever little adult, nearly on a par with them. But Don Rice was a mystery man to me. Not only had he never spoken, he had never even looked my way. Gradually he became, in my mind, almost mythic. Almost satanic. I had grown afraid of this stealthy keeper of the garden.

One evening in the swing my mother asked, "Son, would you like to go up to Jake's Restaurant and get some ice cream for you kids?" No, I would not, I thought.

Jake Savage's concrete-block establishment, across from Wurts Chinn's, was brand new and totally unfamiliar to me. I knew only that it catered to teenagers. That concerned me. Still, the idea of ice cream grew stronger until I consented to the journey. My mother gave me the necessary money, and I crossed the highway and started toward the restaurant.

Rock-'n'-roll music blared from Jake's jukebox. The song was "Alley Oop." I thought of my Uncle Willard, who lived nearby and who only last week had complained about the loudness of that very tune as it played over and over while he struggled to sleep before going out on midnight shift at the Raceland C & O Car Shops. "Alley Oop, oop, oop, oop, oop-oop, Alley Oop, oop, oop, oop, oop-oop."

I began to see my uncle's point. Somehow, Early Man as the

topic of a pop song seemed incongruous and grotesque. Foreboding. Further, I had begun to worry about the business transaction associated with the ice cream. Certainly I had bought items in the grocery stores many times already, but now I was dealing with a different kind of place. I fretted: Was I supposed to pay the waitress before or after she served me the cones? Worse yet, should I give her change or would she give me change?

Approaching the girl behind the dairy-cream window screen, I could see inside the restaurant, where all manner of late adolescents danced and laughed around the concrete floor. Particularly appalling to me were the boys' Hollywood flat-top haircuts, along with their nearly fluorescent, pastel-colored pants and white-buck shoes. This was not my territory. The teens whirled around en masse like a group of wayward Puritans at a maypole, and there in the middle of it all I saw my Uncle Scott. He had joined the Fallen Angels. My faith was gone.

"Can I help you, honey," the pink-uniformed girl said as she popped her chewing gum. She struck me as an exotic creature, such a pretty thing if not so charming. Yet she was not actually paying much attention to me, because she and her fellow waitress were in an erudite discussion as to whether the song now playing inside was properly called "Honeycomb" or "Honeycone". To her credit, she favored the former pronunciation.

Meanwhile I had decided to hold tight to my money until the right moment seized me. So I nervously ordered and stood outside, hoping for the best. The girl filled three sugar cones from a metal cylinder, set each of them into slots in a cardboard container of four-cone capacity, slid back the window and handed it all to me.

Perhaps because of the odd number of items in the box, and most surely because of my shakiness in such a foreign situation, one of the cones spilled out onto the gravels at my feet. Stunned and enraged, I could see nothing but blackness. I threw the container and both the other cones against the side of the building, then hurled all the money in my other hand through the open window. I began running alongside the highway, hearing the cries and admonitions of everyone sitting in their swings across from me—"Charlotte, get your boy, he's a-loose from the dairy queen!"—but virtually sightless from hard crying.

Coming upon the apple orchard, I climbed to a plank atop the fence and paused. *Don't ever get over into Don Rice's field.* I jumped inside the pasture and headed straight for the trees, hugging the first one I came to, burying my head against its rough, brown, soothing bark, where I remained until a strange hand touched my shoulder and gently led me through the orchard gate and into my mother's arms. Enormous relief replaced my great humiliation.

Nowadays the old neighborhood, which I left many years ago, is radically changed. Don Rice's orchard has been replaced by a trailer park. Still, whenever I have had my fill of modern life's social and technical demands, I take to the trees. Apple, when available.

The Wurtland Merchants

"Wurtland's feat of stepping into the League and knocking off both Russell and Huntington is the talk of the fast little circuit, and managers today were checking their schedules with alarm as the Greenup County team looms menacingly ahead."

— *The Ashland Daily Independent*, June 7, 1937

The little river port of Wurtland, situated in northeastern Kentucky, has always been a town of industrial workers, beginning with the arrival of the Pennsylvania iron masters in the 1840s and continuing with the establishment of the Russell Division of the C & O Railway in 1886. In the early decades of this century, the game of baseball spread to Wurtland and thousands of other small towns as it began appealing more and more to the common man, thus enjoying a truly national popularity.

By the 1930s, with the onset of the Great Depression and its woes, the Sunday afternoon clash between Wurtland's ball club and those of rival towns had become an established, perhaps even necessary tradition. The bleak, grim times demanded an outlet for the people, and baseball offered itself as a panacea. As Robert W. Creamer writes in *BASEBALL: An Illustrated History*:

> There wasn't a lot of money around in the Depression years, and the lack of money gave the game a measure of intimacy, a kinship with the people that it hadn't had before and hasn't had since. More than ever, baseball reflected the times.

The dusty old ball field by Savage's Pond hosted many a well-played fray from the time of the Wallstreet Panic to the advent of World War II. My father, Monte Holt, recalls that the crowds in attendance generally consisted of "a handful of men standing around under the shade of some peach trees, loafing, and sometimes a couple of the married players' wives would show up. Of course, there weren't many people back then anyway. And there was nothing fancy about the playing field. No baseball fence in the outfield. They did think to put a backstop in front of the pond, though."

Despite the humble setting, Delbert Enyart of Wurtland remembered "some real ballplayers, I'll tell you. Other teams went all over the country and recruited players they thought could beat us. But we still won." In a moment of unbridled enthusiasm, oldtimer Bud Young concurred: "Why, we coulda beat the Cincinnati Redlegs, couldn't we, Deb!"

Towns providing opposition for Wurtland were Princess, Louisa, Cannonsburg, Willard, Stinson, Olive Hill, Melrose, Fullerton, and McDermott and Portsmouth, the latter two based in Ohio. "We used to catch the train called the Accommodation at seven o'clock in the morning, ride down to Fullerton, play a ballgame, then ride back home on the five o'clock run," said Enyart.

Enyart's father, Laban, was one of Wurtland's outstanding players in the early 30s. A stout man built along the lines of turn-of-the-century pitching great Cy Young, Labe Enyart was a right-handed "underslinger" whose offspeed deliveries baffled hitters. He had actually begun pitching in the 20s with a strong C & O team that traveled as far away as Columbus, Ohio, and Charlottesville, Virginia. Often he had pitched and won both ends of a doubleheader, once lasting through a total of twenty-two innings in one afternoon.

During his last years as Wurtland's pitcher, Labe's "warm-up" catcher before games and between innings was my father, who still remarks on the "heaviness" of the ball as he received it in his mitt: "It looked so slow coming up to the plate, but it just about tore my left hand off to catch it."

Another prominent early performer, Everett Griffith, was by profession, and perhaps out of necessity, a hobo. Said Deb Enyart, "He would catch a train on Sunday evening after a ballgame and wear his ball suit all week, riding in boxcars, but he'd be back the next Sunday in time for the game."

Equally colorful was Herschel "Hog" Cochran, a big, fun-loving right-handed pitcher with a style similar to that of the famed St. Louis Cardinal hurler, Dizzy Dean. The possessor of a ferocious fastball, "Hoggy" worked over both the opposing batters and his own catcher every time he took the mound. "His hat flew off on every pitch," my father declared, "and he had no idea where the ball was going, but he could throw it through the side of a tobacco barn."

Perhaps the finest hitter ever to play for Wurtland was strong, silent Doyle Chinn, a left-handed first baseman who, according to Deb Enyart, "hit the longest ball we ever saw out of the old field. It went over a barbed-wire pasture fence in right-center field. I can safely say it went at least 400 feet, maybe 450, before it hit the ground." Added local wag Estill Maggard, "Boys, it sailed far and beyond."

The early teams were sponsored and managed by storekeeper Wurts Chinn, and a roll call of other outstanding talents includes Hog Cochran's excellent battery mate, Kenner Braden; steady shortstop John Dickerson; and bunting specialist and speedy center fielder Gib Owens. In addition, there was catcher Mayo Boggs, as well as infielders Deb Enyart, Bud Young, Raymond Adams and Frank Williams; first basemen Alva Savage and George Chinn; outfielders Herschel Ealey, Emory Fannin and Curt Boggs; and pitchers Woody Evans and John McCarty.

In one particularly crucial game, big first sacker George Chinn came to bat in a rather heavily inebriated condition. He nevertheless promptly hit a tremendous drive that rolled to the base of Bob Savage's barn in left field. As Chinn rounded third base, the excitement of the moment combined with his heady physical state, and he stumbled over the bag, staggered, and sprawled vaingloriously into the dirt. Fortunately, two alert and partisan bystanders--Van Boggs and Harlan Fritz—managed to dash out and drag the bewildered slugger across home plate just ahead of the third relay throw from the barn.

It was also Van Boggs who, in 1932, accompanied the Wurtland team on a road trip to Olive Hill, forty miles away, and was charged 35 cents to enter the ballpark. Since an admission price was unheard of in the league at the time, Boggs became insulted and miffed. Added to his frustration was the seeming lack of a drink of water anywhere around the dusty, drought-ridden diamond. As he paced beside the foul lines that afternoon with his parched throat burning, Boggs began a lament that became standard from then on with the Wurtland faithful: "Thirty-five cents and no water in Olive Hill, Kentucky!"

From 1937 through 1939, the team known as the Greenup County Merchants became a highly successful and popular crew, making their mark in both the Northeastern Kentucky and Tri-State Leagues. Existing records show the Merchants compiling a winning percentage of .760 while gaining several playoff victories and capturing a couple of league championships.

The highly competitive Tri-State League included three West Virginia franchises: Barboursville, Ceredo-Kenova and Huntington; two Ohio teams: Ironton C & O and Ramey's Feed of Portsmouth; and four Kentucky teams: the Flatwoods Eagles, Schenker's Market of Russell, Ashland Pure Milk, and the Merchants of Wurtland.

Directed by player-manager Bill Harrell, the Merchants were led by lanky pitcher Lawrence Maddox, who won more than eighty per cent of his decisions; catcher Earl Mowery, a swift lead-off man; steady third baseman Jimmy Kirk; the hard-hitting, rangy cousin combination of Hollis Heaberlin at shortstop and Harold Heaberlin at second base; and center fielder Grandin Chinn, a fleet flyhawk whose steady improvement at the plate warranted him tryouts with the St. Louis Cardinals at their camps in Portsmouth, Ohio, in 1937 and Albany, Georgia, in 1938.

In fact, Chinn and future World Series stars Whitey Kurowski, Johnny Hopp, Ernie White and Hall of Fame great Stan "The Man" Musial worked out together under the stern scrutiny of legendary general manager Branch Rickey. "I was the last man released both years," Chinn wistfully recalled. In addition to the local boys, several players from the neighboring towns of Greenup and Raceland, as well as from southeastern Ohio, joined the Merchants and took Sunday dinner at the home of Wurts and Addie Chinn before performing in the afternoon doubleheaders.

So those were the players and the teams, and those days are longtime gone now; but in a sense, baseball—at least as a game in the mind—never leaves the true fan. As Roger Angell writes in his novel *The Summer Game*:

> Baseball's time is seamless and invisible,
> A bubble within which players move at exactly
> The same pace and rhythms as their predecessors.
>
> This is the way the game was played in our youth
> And in our father's youth, and even back then,
> Back in the country days, there must have been
> This same feeling that time could be stopped.

Today, in my own mind, I can easily imagine a serene, confident Lawrence Maddox standing on the pitcher's mound, his cap cocked over his right eye, peering in to the swarthy Earl Mowery for his signal, then slowly winding and whipping a sibilant strike past a startled batter to end another game at the old Wurtland field.

About the Author

A native of Wurtland, Kentucky, Stephen M. Holt is a graduate of Eastern Kentucky University, where he earned a bachelor's degree in English, and Morehead State University, where he completed a major in French as well as masters' degrees in English and secondary education. He has taught for twenty-nine years in the Russell (KY) Independent School System, and for well over a decade as part-time instructor at Ohio University's Southern Campus in Ironton. Recipient of Ashland Inc.'s Golden Apple Achiever Award for Distinguished Teaching, he has also been honored numerous times by students in the Kentucky Governor's Scholars Program.

Holt lives in Raceland, Kentucky, where he shares his home with wife Linda and miniature poodle Kismet. A daughter, Chaille Brook Ahumada, resides in Fuquay-Varina, North Carolina, with husband Guillermo.